BRIDEGROOM and BRIDE

BRIDEGROOM *and* BRIDE

RONALD KNOX

ಊಲ

CLUNY
Providence, Rhode Island

CLUNY MEDIA EDITION, 2022

For more information regarding this title
or any other Cluny Media publication,
please write to info@clunymedia.com, or to
Cluny Media, P.O. Box 1664, Providence, RI 02901

VISIT US ONLINE AT WWW.CLUNYMEDIA.COM

Bridegroom and Bride copyright © Lady Magdalen Howard 1957

Published by permission.

Cluny Media edition copyright © 2022 Cluny Media LLC

ISBN: 978-1685951580

ALL RIGHTS RESERVED

Nihil obstat: Joannes M. T. Barton, S.T.D., L.S.S., *Censor Deputatus*

Imprimatur: Georgius L. Craven, *Epus Sebastopolis*, Vic. Cap. Westmon.
WESTMONASTERII, DIE 23A NOV. 1956

Cover design by Clarke & Clarke
Cover image: Henri Martin, *The Lovers*,
date unknown, oil on canvas
Courtesy of Wikimedia Commons

CONTENTS

PREFACE		i
CHAPTER 1.	*Here Present*	1
CHAPTER 2.	*I Will*	5
CHAPTER 3.	*I Take Thee*	9
CHAPTER 4.	*To Have and to Hold*	15
CHAPTER 5.	*I Thee Wed*	21
CHAPTER 6.	*With My Body*	27
CHAPTER 7.	*The Threefold Invocation*	33
CHAPTER 8.	*Confirma Hoc Deus*	39
CHAPTER 9.	*The Nuptial Mass*	45
CHAPTER 10.	*The Nuptial Blessing*	51
CHAPTER 11.	*The Christmas Present*	55
CHAPTER 12.	*Our Lady's Yes*	61
CHAPTER 13.	*The Fruitful Vine*	65
CHAPTER 14.	*The Joyful Parting*	71
CHAPTER 15.	*To Prepare a Home*	77
CHAPTER 16.	*Veni, Sancte Spiritus*	83
CHAPTER 17.	*The Easy Yoke*	89

CHAPTER 18. *Nihil Fortius Amore*   95

CHAPTER 19. *St. Mary on the Quay*   99

CHAPTER 20. *On the Palms of My Hands*   105

CHAPTER 21. *His Own Sheep*   111

CHAPTER 22. *Leading-Strings of Love*   115

CHAPTER 23. *The True Vision*   119

CHAPTER 24. *Life More Abundantly*   123

To Toni Lothian
who first suggested this book

PREFACE

༄༅

SOME YEARS AGO, I WAS ASKED TO PREACH AT A fashionable wedding. The bridegroom told me, with admirable candour, exactly what he wanted: "You know— the kind of thing for which five minutes is too short, and ten minutes is too long." Since he was the Earl Marshal of England, I was ready to trust his judgement in these matters of protocol; and I have, I think, scrupulously observed his ruling whenever I have been called upon, since then, to perform the same office. These occasions have been fairly numerous; when you have been chaplain to undergraduates for thirteen years, and lived for four years under the same roof with a convent school, a certain nupturiency among your friends is only to be expected. And I have preached, always, a new sermon. There are, to be sure, fish-slices which have done duty at several weddings in their time, but the precedent was not one to be followed; friendship seemed to demand that an address of this kind should be specially composed, and torn up in the sacristy.

Well, not exactly torn up; I have a horror of destroying things. If the gourmet preserves old menu-cards, to remind him of past banquets, I must be pardoned for treasuring up these mementoes, each recalling moments of great happiness which I was privileged to share. Now and again, in turning out my drawers, I found that they were sitting up ominously, and at last decided to give them that form of burial which befits one's own faded manuscripts—publication. In embalming them, I have been careful to obliterate all such tailor's marks as might betray the identity of the people concerned. Those to whom they properly belong will find themselves commemorated here only as Titius and Bertha.

The reader, however, must not expect to be presented with a complete *Tractatus de Matrimonio*. The somewhat narrow limits prescribed to me (as I have said) by an unimpeachable authority made methodical treatment impossible. Not for me the full-length, official portrait; picture me rather as the sightseer who climbs up to some point of vantage and takes a snap-shot of the happy pair as they leave the church. Now the scene of the ceremony, now some feast in the calendar, now some phrase in the

Bridegroom and Bride

wedding service itself, would give me my starting-point. And yet, now that I have collected them in an album, these views, taken at random, have a kind of unity about them; a unity in diversity, perhaps—but what else is marriage?

Or say, if you will, that I have rung the changes on a set of commonplace truths; obvious enough, and yet, because of our human frailty, not seldom obscured.

R. A. Knox
Mells, 1956

CHAPTER I

Here Present

*Lord, thou hast been our refuge from
generation to generation.* (Ps. 89:1)

IT IS DUE, I SUPPOSE, TO THE ENORMOUS INSTINCT of Holy Church for legalities, that the bride and bridegroom were asked, a few moments ago, "Dost thou take So-and-so, *here present*?" There must be no question, later, of an annulment on the ground that they really meant to marry two other people of the same name. But the wedding ceremony has such a fairy-like trick of turning everything to gold, even the most commonplace things, that those words "here present" always take on, for me, the colours of romance. I like to imagine that there is a feeling of tense excitement till the last moment as to whether the bride will really turn up; until at last the priest (may I put it like that, in this company?) calls

RONALD KNOX

absence—"A.B." "Here, Father." "C.D." "Here, Father." "Good, then we can start." Alternatively, it might be a sort of drawing-room game, in which either of you was expected to choose a partner from among *all* the persons here present; only there was collusion, and you two arranged beforehand to choose each other. But best of all, we might think of the priest as addressing you in that way because you are the *only* persons really present. The priest himself is only a voice booming out unnecessary questions, and everybody else is miles away; you two stand there alone with each other, alone in your earthly Paradise, fenced off with flaming swords.

And the best of it is that you will—I mean that you can—I mean that you can with God's blessing—I mean that you will with God's blessing, be always like that. The ring is to be a fairy ring this time, and you two are to be struck, permanently, in the attitude in which you stand now, present in a special way to one another; present to one another in that special way, even when you are in the presence of other people; smiling at us others, laughing with us, helping us, sympathizing with us, but all the time shut away together in a world-proof isolation which you have made for yourselves by love. We, your friends, want to stand always a little in the background, as we stand now, so that we may never disturb or distract

Bridegroom and Bride

that perfect fellowship in which you are present to one another henceforward.

Is it all only a fairy-tale? That ring, we know, is not in fact charged with any magical properties; it is good honest gold, no more. It will last a life-time; but the love which it symbolizes and seals, will that (the cynic wants to know) last a life-time? Is it even wise for us, your friends, to encourage you in romantic sentiments about it, instead of telling you to look out on the future in a cooler, a more prosaic spirit? I do not see how such language can be held, such thoughts entertained, by Christian people. For that solitude of two which you build for yourselves will not, after all, envelop you wholly; you are present to one another in the presence of God. That presence wraps us around like the air we breathe, is the medium in which all the good we know maintains itself and flourishes. And you two, supported not only by your love for one another, but by a common faith in the loveliest of all religions, how should you not integrate those two experiences? Divine and human love are not strangers to one another, are not forces pulling in different directions. All the sacramental life you share can but reawaken in you the grace of the sacrament you have received today. And your love for one another will flow back into your spiritual lives, deepening and strengthening your love for

RONALD KNOX

Jesus Christ. Your love grow less? Not while it is fed by the power that multiplied the loaves, and turned water into wine. Incarnate Christ does not fail to take all that is most human in us and divinize it.

Here present—for you, here and now present, in this unforgettable moment, a link has been forged that will last a life-time. And those of us who are privileged to witness, today, the forging of such a link in a second generation of this family, must be pardoned if our minds travel back to a wedding ceremony performed thirty-one years ago, with gratitude for God's mercies, and with a sense of auspicious association. "Lord, thou hast been our refuge from generation to generation"; may that protecting care that has watched over this house watch over it still. And when you two, thirty-one years hence, look back to the ceremony of today, may you be still present to one another, in your thoughts, in your prayers, in the sanctities of your home, and at God's altar. May the prayers of our blessed Lady and St. Joseph go with you, to hallow your joys, and comfort your sorrows; may they win for you perfect trust in one another, and perfect trust in the God who has joined you to one another, our refuge from generation to generation.

CHAPTER 2

I Will

Vain is the builder's toil, if the house is not of the Lord's building. (Ps. 126:1)

WE HAVE JUST HEARD PRONOUNCED, FIRST BY A man's voice, then by a woman's, what is perhaps the shortest significant sentence in the English language; it consisted only of five letters, only of two words, "I will." Yet the significance of it is curiously profound. In using it, you assert, after a double manner, your freedom. You are not compelled by any inner necessity of your own nature; a beast cannot choose in a decision of whatever importance, it may be, in finding a mate, it can only follow the law of its own instinct. But man chooses; he says, "I will." Again, you are not subject to any compulsion on the part of your fellow men; you are a free citizen. You are not being directed by the State into such and such a marriage, as you might be directed by the State into such and such a form of employment. It is by an act of free consent that you say, "I will."

And then, after doubly asserting their freedom, man and woman, in our presence, have renounced their freedom. They have signed away their liberties by undertaking a life-long engagement to each other.

Is that a strange proceeding? On the contrary, it is part of our everyday experience that you cannot enter into any fruitful partnership without some abridgement of your own freedom, without some renunciation of your own will for the sake of the common good. To this day, the problem which chiefly exercises our statesmen is that, and no other. How far can the nations of Western Europe unite to secure peace and recovery, without abrogating their own national sovereignties? That is the law of all association; what wonder that it should hold good in that closest of all human associations, the home? All the time, husband and wife must be playing up to one another; not by heroic sacrifice, but by a thousand little acts of daily considerateness; that is the mortar by which the house stands.

Is it possible? Can two human beings really live under the same roof, day after day, month after month, without a hopeless clash of personalities? It would be impossible,

Bridegroom and Bride

we all know, if it were not for that strange talisman we call love. "Love," says the author of the *Imitation*, "makes things burdensome light to carry, bears evenly the uneven weight; burden so borne, burden is none, nor any bitterness but becomes sweet to the taste…No weight love feels, no labour counts laborious; ever ready to go beyond its powers, calling no task impossible; it knows no language but *I can* and *I may*. It has strength for every undertaking, performs every duty, brings all to accomplishment, where he that is no lover faints and falls by the way." Such a talisman is yours, and you ask in bewilderment how you could need anything more than this, anything different from this?

More than this? No. Different from this? No. That is not what we mean when we tell you that you need the grace of this sacrament, to confirm your resolution, to transform your *I will* into *I do*. Grace is not something that comes in from the outside, and says, "No, you are doing it wrong, let me show you how to do it." Grace is not a kind of auxiliary steam, supplementing our feeble powers with a force not of the same character. Grace does not replace nature, it perfects nature, transmutes something that belongs to earth and makes it glow with the radiance of heaven. And nowhere is that more clear than in the Sacrament of Matrimony. The love which you feel for one another is already something sacramental; it is the raw material, the uncut jewel waiting for the divine action to polish it. Not something more, not something different; but that same love, only stronger, only deeper, only more supernaturally enduring.

"I will"—did it surprise us that those words, with their assertion of human liberty, should at the same time be used to sign your liberty away? We were wrong; our liberty is given to us so that we may accept the service of God, that service which is perfect freedom. And you, in accepting one another, have accepted God's will for you; it was his will that you should achieve your sanctification together, each sanctified by that way of married life which is at once a revelation of love, and an opportunity of service. Your "I will," and yours, echoed that perfect act of submission which our blessed Lady made when she said, "Let it be unto me according to thy word." May her prayers, and the prayers of St. Joseph, build your house for you; enable you to find, in the sanctities of married life, the opportunity to serve God in your generation; may they bring you at last to that eternal wedding feast, where there is no more parting, and the love which was imaged to us here on earth will be perfectly made known.

CHAPTER 3

I Take Thee

*Give, and gifts will be yours; good measure,
pressed down and shaken up and running over,
will be poured into your lap.* (LUKE 6:38)

WHAT A SELFISH THING THE WEDDING CEREMONY seems, at first sight! "Wilt thou take? ... I will. Wilt thou take? I will. I, A.B., take thee, C.D. I, C.D., take thee, A.B." It seems to be all taking and no giving. To be sure, gold and silver change hands; and there is some talk of endowment with worldly goods, a liturgical echo of the marriage settlement. But something more important than gold and silver has changed hands, two human lives. Two people have claimed one another, by some special right of acquisition, carried one another off, left a gap, two gaps, in the circle of their friends. And then they levy blackmail on us, in the form of wedding-presents,

RONALD KNOX

to celebrate their triumph. Is it fitting that such acquisitiveness, such possessiveness should be applauded, and applauded in the name of religion?

The answer to our difficulty is that this ceremony is not really one of taking; it is only our use of lawyer's language that gives us that impression; it is really a ceremony of giving. Marriage, on either side, is self-surrender. Bride and bridegroom minister the sacrament to one another, not so much by accepting, each in turn, the gift made, as by standing there in silence and making, each in turn, the gift that is being accepted. What we applaud, we who stand by, is not the taking but the making of the gift; for giving is the essence of love. We say, don't we, when one of our friends makes a marriage we don't approve of, that So-and-so has thrown himself, or herself, away. But in saying that we do not impress the lover; the lover always wants to throw himself, or herself, away; it is the very technique of love. You must want to surrender yourself and live for somebody else, if true love is to be distinguished from that contemptible thing, which is its counterfeit. We come here to congratulate you, each of you, on a prize won. But, more importantly, we come here, in times when giving is out of fashion, to see two people throw themselves away.

Not that it seems so to you; how should it? You are only conscious of a prize won; not of giving anything.

Bridegroom and Bride

That is as it should be; we give best when we do not know that we are giving. To live for others instead of living for oneself—how difficult that is to us fallen creatures, how laboriously such results are produced in us by the grace of Christ working in the depths of the soul! But with lovers it is different; with them, grace rises to the surface; grace and nature, instead of being two opposed forces that pull in two different directions, pull together for once; natural affection and supernatural charity find, for once, the same object and the same field of activity. In this sacrament, more obviously than in any other, nature is supernaturalized, becomes the handmaid of grace. Unselfishness, for you two, is not a tardy effort of the will, it is a spontaneous reaction; may it ever remain so! For this unselfishness which love sets up in us is not meant to be a passing phase which lives and dies with youth; it looks forward to the setting up of a Christian home, and the bringing up, if it be God's will, of a Christian family. Unselfishness in husband and wife takes on a new colour, finds a new outlet, when it is seen as unselfishness in father and mother; it strikes out into the future, is made one with God's will for the continuance of our race. God knows we wish you happiness; but we wish you first unselfishness, and happiness as the fruit of it.

Give, and gifts will be yours—does that mean that

RONALD KNOX

unselfishness is always rewarded in this world, that if we are generous in our dealings with others, we shall, as a matter of course, be treated generously in return? Experience, alas, does not bear out that interpretation of the passage; nor, I think, would that interpretation be in line with the tenor of our Lord's teaching. He does not recommend generosity to us as a kind of enlightened self-interest. And perhaps the best commentary on this utterance of his is another utterance of his which has not been preserved in the Gospels; it has come down to us, by a providential accident, in a speech of St. Paul's. "Remembering the words spoken by the Lord Jesus himself, 'It is more blessed to give than to receive.'" More blessed, beyond doubt, in the sense that we shall be rewarded hereafter. But these future rewards cast their shadow beforehand; even in this world, it is true as a general thing that the unselfish people are the better off for it, because the source of their happiness lies in themselves, not in outward circumstances which may play them false. Enjoy your felicity; God means us to enjoy his gifts. But pray, each of you, for an increase of that unselfishness which lies, without your knowing it, at the roots of your enjoyment. The cynic will tell you that married happiness is a matter of give and take. Do not believe him; it is a matter of give and give.

Bridegroom and Bride

May our blessed Lady and St. Joseph, that are friendly to all true lovers, win such grace for your wedding that you may live, each of you, as they did, each of them, for one another; that you may live, both of you, as they did, both of them, for Jesus Christ.

CHAPTER 4

To Have and to Hold

You must be servants still, serving one another in a spirit of charity. (GAL. 5:13)

THE WEDDING SERVICE IS A VERY SHORT ONE, occupying about ten minutes. It seems about five minutes to the congregation at large; the bride and bridegroom have the impression that it has lasted about three quarters of an hour. This is partly nervousness; but partly because the congregation have only caught the words that are put down in the ritual, whereas the bride and bridegroom have been listening all the time to the priest putting in a series of stage directions in a rapid undertone. They have forgotten everything they learned up beforehand, and find themselves obeying the priest in a mood of dazed acquiescence. But there is one point at which they always register a dumb protest. When the

RONALD KNOX

bridegroom has pronounced the words "and thereto I plight thee my troth," the priest says *sotto voce*: "Now let go one another's hands," and, when they have done so: "Now join your hands again." I have never yet seen bride and bridegroom whose eyes did not register the protest: "Then why on earth did you tell us to let go?" But it is not that the priest has made a mistake; it is all down in the ritual.

There must be a reason for it; and the reason, I have always thought, must be this. To the bride and bridegroom, the plighting of troth seems a mere formality; they have rehearsed that part a hundred times before. The love that binds them is something shared, a current which passes from one to the other, so that the man's giving of himself to the woman, and the woman's giving of herself to the man, seems to them but a single act. If it were not for grammatical difficulties, they would prefer to make the declaration jointly, in the first person plural, which is the language of love. They are already one; bridegroom takes bride by the hand, bride takes bridegroom—it is all one thing; why make two bites of a cherry?

But the Church, with that uncomfortable realism which is so characteristic of her, sees the situation differently. They are not yet sacramentally one; they are two separate people, by each of whom, independently, a

Bridegroom and Bride

lifelong undertaking must be given. "My children," she says, "you are still two persons, not one, and I want an assurance, not from both of you, but from each of you. It refers, not simply to this moment of blissful surrender, but to the ups and downs of a whole lifetime. Each takes the other 'in sickness or in health'; and you will not both be having influenza at the same time. One of you will be depressed, fractious, irritable; to the other, that will be a test of love and an opportunity of service. That you are both in love with one another, I know well enough. But I want the assurance that each of you means to serve the other, come what may. That is a separate responsibility for each of you; so, you first, your hand in hers, and then you, your hand in his."

"You must be servants still" the Apostle tells us, "serving one another"—or we might translate it, quite literally, "you must be slaves still, enslaved to one another." In ancient Rome, when the master acquired a new slave, he took him by the hand; that is how we get our word "emancipation." And in doing so, he said: "I affirm that by the law of the city this man is mine." Well, we have just seen that ceremony repeated; persisting, I suppose, after all these centuries. Only, as usual, the law of Christ has turned the whole significance of the ceremony upside down. "I take thee, to have and to hold"; the formula is still one of taking, but the sense is one of giving; either party in using it becomes, not acquires, a slave. We Christians, free with that liberty with which Christ has emancipated us, are still the slaves of charity; whoever has need of the service I can give him becomes, by that fact, my master.

And you two have accepted that Christian duty, within the narrow circle of which the wedding ring is the symbol. Not that you have shaken off your responsibility as Christian people for serving others at need; you have not shut yourselves off in a little world of your own. No, but the sun's rays, that warm the whole world of nature, may be focused with a burning-glass in such a way that the greatest power of them is concentrated in a single spot. And your wedding ring is your burning-glass, concentrating the rays of your charity on a single spot, your home. How ready we are, we scandal-loving human creatures, to make the most of any little disagreement between man and wife! But if only there were more simplicity about us, we should watch, with admiration and gratitude, all the little marks of attention husband and wife show to one another, all the little offices they perform for one another, as an encouragement and a model to us all. May the prayers of our blessed Lady and St. Joseph make your home a burning focus of willing

Bridegroom and Bride

self-sacrifice, for us others to warm our hands at, in days when charity has grown cold.

CHAPTER 5

I Thee Wed

All mine, and I all his. (CANT. 2:16)

THE RITE OF MATRIMONY PRESCRIBED BY OUR English ritual, and the rite prescribed by the Book of Common Prayer, are, in their central features, almost indistinguishable. Not because either is copied from the other, but because both derive, with little alteration, from the Middle Ages. The Elizabethan service-books changed so much, but the wedding service hardly at all. How the Puritans longed to abolish the ring, as a piece of manifest idolatry! But the ring was not abolished. And meanwhile, for two centuries, those who followed the old religion must go to school abroad, derive their inspiration from abroad, adopt French or Italian ways of doing things; somewhere, sometime, you would have expected them to pick up a new marriage rite. But no; all through the times of persecution, that didn't change. When you are married at East Hendred, you plight your troth as people plighted their troth at East Hendred five centuries back.

And, as if to drive that home, in the really operative part of the rite the grammar itself gets out of control, and carries us back to the very origins of the language. "I thee wed...I thee worship...I thee endow"—not: "I wed thee, I worship thee, I endow thee." This is not the English which you read in the Book of Common Prayer; still less is it the English of our modern vernacular devotions. It comes down to us from medieval times, when the English language was still fluid, not yet hardened in a mould, and they kept the order of the words in the Latin. "I thee wed, I thee worship, I thee endow"—by a fortunate accident, this unstudied effect of language adds, to the beauty of the wedding service, a beauty of its own. "I thee"—the two pronouns are now so closely united that not even a verb may come between them. "I thee"—as if the bridegroom were so overcome by the strength of his own feelings that he cannot wait to express himself in coherent English; he can only stammer out, as it comes to him, the language of a lover. "I thee"—all the emphasis thrown upon one word, because that word is the magnet which draws all his attention to itself.

Only the bridegroom uses that phrase; the bride,

Bridegroom and Bride

once the ring has been blessed, remains silent, the passive recipient of grace. But we do not doubt that her heart echoes it; she, too, is for wedding; she, too, is body and soul for him; she too gives, and gives what is not to be valued in terms of gold and silver, her life's happiness. For her, too, it is significant, that instinctive juxtaposition of pronouns; he is next to her heart, as she to his.

"I thee"—how is it that two human beings, with all the frailty of our human nature, all the uncertainty of our human destiny before their eyes, have the courage to put their happiness in one another's keeping? That terrifying book, the *Imitation of Christ*, has something discouraging to say about it, as usual. "If you tie up your peace of mind," it says, "with any human creature, under the impression that you can think common thoughts and live a common life, you will always be restless, always bound hand and foot." We all of us have our good and our bad times; pounds, shillings, and pence are a matter of constant solicitude; the mechanism of our body plays us false very easily; and all these things make it difficult for us to serve God as we would like to, with complete steadiness of purpose, complete freedom of action. How, then, can man venture to take woman, woman take man, for better for worse, for richer for poorer, in sickness and in health? Is not this to double the distractions which are so ready to come between us and God?

RONALD KNOX

Forgive us, if we seem to overcast the dawn of your happiness with the shadow of a scruple. That it is only a scruple, the first page of human history assures us. He who said: "Let us make man, wearing our own image," went on to say: "It is not well that man should be without companionship." It is revealed to us that we ought not to think of Almighty God himself as reigning in utter loneliness; in the very heart of the Divine Being there is a multiplicity of Persons, mysteriously united by the Holy Spirit, who is Love. And because we wear God's image, it is not natural for man to be alone; it is natural that man should say to woman, "I thee wed, I thee worship, I thee endow, in the name of the Father and of the Son and of the Holy Ghost, Amen." There is, to be sure, a vocation which binds man or woman to loneliness; a vocation which comes to few, of which fewer still are found worthy. But it is natural for man or woman to look out on a world-picture framed in a human companionship; we see better, don't we, with two eyes than with one? And man and woman happily wedded can attain, between them, a clearness of view, a sureness of touch, that would not have come to either of them if they had travelled alone.

That there may be no shadow over this God-given happiness of yours; that the close knitting of "thou" to "I" may be, not just a mood of the moment, but the fixed

Bridegroom and Bride

attitude of a life-time, is the prayer of your friends who have come here to wish you well, is the prayer of the Church as she registers and ratifies the vows that have passed between you. May the anniversary of this your wedding-day bring back to you, always, the memory of a quiet village church, and the thought of that village bride whose name, all through the dark times of history, has been loved and honoured in East Hendred.

CHAPTER 6

With My Body

Youth itself may weaken, the warrior faint and flag,
but those who trust in the Lord will renew
their strength, like eagles new fledged; hasten
and never grow weary of hastening, march on
and never weaken on the march. (ISA. 40:30–31)

WHEN TWO CATHOLICS GET MARRIED IN THE United States of America, the rite they use differs in some respects from ours. The ring has been blessed, and the bridegroom must put it on the bride's finger; what does he say in doing so? "With this ring I thee wed, and I plight unto thee my troth." That, and nothing more. That no gold and silver should change hands, that there should be no talk of endowing her with his worldly goods, is no matter; the lawyers will see to that; but he has made one other omission. "With my body I thee worship"—that phrase has disappeared. A marriage rite composed to meet twentieth-century needs differs in this from a pre-Reformation rite like our own; it will ignore, with a kind of nervous embarrassment, the existence of sex. "With my body I thee worship"—there could be no more delicate recognition of the fact that we are soul and body at once; even the grosser element in man must pay homage to the mystery that is here. Our modern ideas will have the body kept in the background; worship is of the soul.

But we *are* body and soul. Body and soul are not two separate territories, meeting and touching, like England and Scotland, at some recognizable frontier. No, the link between them is so subtle and so elusive that the ablest of scientists cannot define it, the subtlest of philosophers cannot explain it; they interpenetrate one another, interact upon one another, beyond our knowing. And in the sacraments Almighty God has supplied us with means of grace by which (since we are body and soul at once) the body can be the actual channel through which a virtue and an influence take possession of the soul. It is hard for us to understand that; but it becomes easier if we concentrate our attention on one particular sacrament, the sacrament we have been celebrating this morning.

Bridegroom and Bride

Matrimony, you see, is a kind of natural sacrament; its office is to irradiate human love with the colours of that which is divine. Yet that human love which is the subject-matter and the raw material of it, is already after a fashion sacramental. Just as you cannot say with confidence, "Here body ends and soul begins," you cannot say with confidence, speaking of two lovers, "Here was a physical, and here was a spiritual attraction." The two threads are intertwined; the body becomes the vehicle of the soul's initiative, touch of hand, glance of eye, can express meaning between lovers, more eloquently than speech. And when they come before the altar to plight their troth irrevocably, either worships in the other not a spirit merely, but a thing of flesh and blood; a face studied in light and shadow, the accents of a familiar voice.

Only, as we know, the partnership between body and soul is an unequal partnership. The soul is unaging, the body is subject to laws of growth and decay. Perhaps the saddest and the most beautiful line in heathen literature is that which the poet sent to his mistress with the present of a garland, Ἀνθεῖς καὶ λήγεις και ου καὶ ὁ στέφανος, "Flower they and fade, garland and girl alike." In this life, the beauty and the ardours of youth are impermanent; and a love which is all of the body, not of the soul, soon becomes a thing of yesterday. But lovers who love with body and soul need fear for no such limitations of their romance; "those who trust in the Lord will renew their strength; hasten, and never weary of hastening, march on, and never weaken on the march."

"With my body I thee worship"—you, her children, come to Mother Church and ask for her blessing on your marriage. And she falls in with your mood; the words of troth-plighting which she dictates to you only just stop short of idolatry. She knows what you are feeling; how you wish that your moment of mortal happiness could be eternal; so strong life beats in you, so whole-hearted the welcome it gives to the call of love. But, with her longer view, she sees this mood of yours as sacramental; this mood of acceptance, in which you claim one another so eagerly. It is the *matter* of a sacrament, signifying and conveying graces of the soul which are deeper and more abiding. Like swimmers carried away by a silent undertow that is too strong for them, you are being swept into the current of that divine love which reaches beyond time and sense; united, beyond your knowing, with that divine will which made you for one another. God will have the worship still.

May the prayers of our blessed Lady and St. Joseph win for your love that supernatural strength which can

Bridegroom and Bride

outlive youth, outlive life itself, ready to be revealed hereafter where life and youth are eternal.

CHAPTER 7

The Threefold Invocation

*That they, too, may be one in us, as thou, Father,
art in me, and I in thee; that while thou art in me,
I may be in them, and so they may perfectly
be made one.* (JOHN 17:21-23)

THE WEDDING SERVICE TO WHICH ENGLISH EARS are attuned, and English minds are accustomed, has remained, beyond example, unaltered through the centuries. There is no important feature in which the Prayer-Book order for the solemnization of matrimony differs from the pre-Reformation ceremony at which we have just assisted. The reason is, I suppose, that English people hold by their social traditions, and a rite so intimately bound up with the common life of English men and women could not be altered without protest. No change was made even in that solemn gesture by which

RONALD KNOX

the bridegroom lets the ring come to rest on the bride's finger, saying, as he does so, "In the name of the Father, and of the Son, and of the Holy Ghost, Amen." Its survival was bitterly resented by the Puritans; you may almost say that this was the issue on which the Civil War was fought, three hundred years back. In the Directory of Public Worship, issued by the Long Parliament, ring and invocation disappeared. But they came back with the Restoration; England was still English.

I say "English" advisedly; if you had got married in the United States of America, the ring would have changed hands, but the three-fold invocation would have been pronounced by the priest, not by the bridegroom. In England, we keep to the old ways; this is the only occasion, I think, upon which the three-fold invocation is uttered in church by a layman. And for a moment it takes our breath away—surely there is something like presumption about it? To you two, pardonably enough, today's ceremony is an epoch in history; time stands still. But in cold fact, is the plighting of troth between man and woman so rare, so momentous an occasion that it should be linked up, thus deliberately, with the central doctrine of the Christian faith? To see the bridegroom bending over the bride's left hand, fumbling as it were over the ceremony and trying first one finger, then the

Bridegroom and Bride

next, until at last the ring finds its home—that is pretty enough, suitable enough. But that, in doing so, he should attach to the thumb and the first two fingers the very names of triune Deity, is not that spell-binding? Were not the Puritans perhaps right, after all, in their determination to get rid of this, the last of the superstitions?

Take courage; you had good reason for what you did. Our Lord himself, in the words I quoted just now, prayed that his true lovers on earth might be one, as he and his Father are one. And when he uses the word "as", he does not refer to some casual resemblance between the two things; how should the warm, sensible experience of earthly love remind us of that bond which unites the three Persons of the Trinity, a thing unimaginable? No, he means that Christian people are to be united with each other on the same principle on which he is united to his Father; their love is to be not merely the echo but the extension of a Love which passes our understanding, because it is divine.

"Ah, but," you say, "he is talking about that bond of good-will which should unite all Christian people, simply because they are Christians, an all-embracing gesture of charity. Why should we suppose that he is thinking of that special intimacy which unites man and woman on their wedding-day, shutting out the rest of the world?

RONALD KNOX

Have we the right so to interpret him?" We have; St. Paul has done so. In a mysterious passage, he tells the Corinthians that "the head to which a wife is united is her husband, just as the head to which every man is united is Christ; so, too, the head to which Christ is united, is God." "As thou, Father, art in me, and I in thee; that while thou art in me, I may be in them, and so they may perfectly be made one"—St. Paul, you see, is adapting that word of his Master's to the circumstances of married life; the charity which binds all Christians together is sacramentally focused in the married love of Christian man and woman, their heads bent over a circlet of gold before God's altar.

And there is no reason to be ashamed of this theological by-play. The bridegroom, in his search for that fourth finger which has less independence of movement than the rest, and so is a fitting symbol of unalterable loyalty, rejects three possibilities, and says to himself, in the words of St. Patrick's breastplate, "I bind unto myself today the strong name of the Trinity." In this atomic age, when the strongest binding force in nature has been wrested apart by man's ingenuity, he can find no analogy in nature for the fidelity with which he loves and is loved; he is driven back on the supernatural. And there he finds, not a mere analogy, but the source and

Bridegroom and Bride

the secret of all love, hidden away in the bosom of the Father.

As man and wife, you will have much in common that is on the ordinary plane of every-day life; little secrets, jokes that are only jokes between you two, memories you share, hopes and ambitions that affect you equally. All that will help to build up your partnership; but behind all that, learn to depend on the grace you have received today; see, always, your marriage vows against a background of mystery. The mystery of Three who are yet One; in whose strength two lives may be lived as one, all the cross-currents of the world notwithstanding.

May the prayers of our blessed Lady and St. Joseph keep your love warm, and make your home a home of rejoicing.

CHAPTER 8

Confirma Hoc Deus

Perfect thy own achievement in us, from
thy holy temple at Jerusalem. (Ps. 67:29-30)

THOSE WORDS, SPOKEN IN LATIN, ARE THE FIRST sound which falls upon the ears of man and woman wedded. The nerve-storm of embarrassment which accompanies the marriage service has attained its peak; the bride has been told which her left hand is, and which her right, and, with the feeling that her left hand does not know what her right hand is doing, has received the gold and silver, has accepted the ring. The bridegroom has said all that he has to say. There is a lull; tension is relaxed. And the Church, at this point, does a rather curious thing. She takes the second half of one verse in the psalms, and the first of the next verse, regardless of the full stop in between, and she makes a single responsory of them—weds them together, you may say, for the sake of the newly-wedded. "Perfect thy own achievement in us, from thy holy temple at Jerusalem."

Forgive me, then, if I avail myself of this lull in the proceedings to interpret, by the space of a few minutes, that prayer which broke from the lips of the Church when she saw the ring finding its home on the ring-finger. She has three things to say. First, that the making of this marriage was God's work, not yours. Next, that it is something achieved, a *fait accompli.* And thirdly, that in spite of that, today's ceremony is not the end of a chapter; it is the beginning of a chapter. The work done needs perfecting.

God wills us, the theologians say, to will freely. A hard saying; yet I could never attend a wedding ceremony without feeling myself to be in the presence of the mystery of grace—that interlocking between God's purposes and ours which underlies all our actions. On the one side, the free will of man and woman is essential to the rite. True, they repeat the words "I will" in a low, strangled voice, as if hypnotized by the insistence of the priest. But the whole context of the situation bears witness to the reality of their consent; as the Lancashire bridegroom said, "Ah coom a'purpose." Here, if anywhere, is deliberate human decision. And yet, that this man and this woman should

Bridegroom and Bride

have met, among all the thousands of their fellows; that each should feel drawn to the other by a mysterious bond whose force they feel, though they cannot analyse its motives—what is this but to be drawn irresistibly by a divine invitation? The achievement of your hopes is the achievement of God's will for you; he meant you for one another, made you for one another.

And it is achievement. The world, for the most part, gives us its prizes so grudgingly and upon such uncertain tenure; permits some of us at last to enjoy the riches that are no use to us, to be loaded with the honours we have ceased to covet; and here are you, so young, so untried in life's battle, rich already in the possession, honoured already in the worship, of one another. Riches and honours are ours only on sufferance; you, by this mutual cession of yourselves, belong to each other. And all that has been effected by a few words muttered, and the passing of a ring.

And yet, is achievement the right word? At least—this is the third point the Church wants us to notice—it is an achievement which admits of, and needs, perfecting. Life is not like a Victorian romance, that it should end with a description of the bridesmaids' dresses; what has been done today, done once for all today, is the first chapter, not the last chapter, in a romance. There is a romance which begins with marriage, less rose-hued, perhaps, as time goes on, but absorbing in its interest. You two are to be the builders of a home, and, please God, of a family; you are to be a fresh unit of Christendom, a fresh cell in its life. Each of you is to be a strength and a consolation to the other, in a world which offers so little strength, so little consolation, to one who travels alone. What we have done today is not merely to be the coping-stone of your betrothal, it is to be the foundation-stone of your married life.

How, then, is it to be perfected, this perfect thing which has been done in you today? The Church, as I have said, boldly plunders the next verse of the psalm to give you a message about that. "From thy holy temple at Jerusalem"—to the Jewish people, in all the vicissitudes of its fortunes, that image of the temple at Jerusalem, high up on the great hills that looked down on the sea-plain, was a symbol of inviolate isolation. The great movements of the world's armies passed it by. And to the Church that same image stands for the supernatural world, so close to ours, interpenetrating ours, and yet so remote from our anxieties. The blessing, then, which she asks for your marriage is that it shall be transformed, by some influence from this supernatural world, into a fortress belonging to you two, rising superior to all the accidents

Bridegroom and Bride

of mortality. We read in the Gospel that St. Joseph and the Blessed Virgin went up every year to Jerusalem; may their intercession make you free citizens, here on earth, of that heavenly Jerusalem, the city of inviolable peace.

CHAPTER 9

The Nuptial Mass

*Look kindly on the sacrifice
we offer thee this day.* (DAN. 3:40)

WHEN WE COME TO GET MARRIED, OUR IMPRESsion is that Holy Church is meeting us, rather unsympathetically, in the spirit of a lawyer. "Oh, you want to get married, do you? Have you been baptized? Where were you baptized? Can you prove that you were baptized? Have you been married before? Can you prove that you haven't been married before?"—and so on. And even when we present ourselves for the ceremony, she insists that the thing shall be done just right; we are confused by a multitude of formalities, just when everything ought to be so simple and so splendid: "*You* stand there...*you* stand there...No, you don't kneel, you stand...Now, put your hand...Not that hand, stupid, the other one"—as if it mattered! And then quite suddenly, when all the registry business is over, she turns to us with a smile and says, "Look; I've got a wedding present for you. You two are going to have a Mass all of your own, all to yourselves."

The nuptial Mass, you see, isn't a Mass said *for* you, like Mass for the sick; it isn't a Mass said *over* you, like Mass for the dead. The nuptial Mass, if I may put it in that way, is said *with* you; it is the accompaniment of your drama, it interprets your emotions. Listen to what the priest is saying, *Introibo ad altare Dei; ad Deum qui laetificat juventutem meam.* "I will go up to the altar of God"—how obvious it sounded, as you heard it day after day; you could *see* that the priest was going up to the altar of God, without being told about it. "The God who gives joy to my youth"—not particularly appropriate, you felt, when the priest, poor old gentleman, was rather rheumatic, and found some difficulty with the altar steps. But today, now that the Mass has become *your* Mass, how it all fits in, takes on a new meaning! Love flies to the altar, because the first instinct of love is sacrifice. You would offer all that you have, immolate all that you are, each for the other; and where, but at God's altar, should that desire find expression? And it is the altar, not of a God who claims, but of a God who gives; the more you seek to annihilate yourselves, the more he bestows on you that joy and youthfulness which are felt, I think, only by lovers.

Bridegroom and Bride

All that, in the very first sentence the priest utters; and all through the Mass it is the same; each mood it reflects is a mood in which you find yourselves. That self-abasement of the *Kyrie eleison*, how natural it seems when either of you feels conscious of having won an undeserved privilege! Even those long silences, which for us others are a pretext for wool-gathering, for you are charged with meaning; as lovers, you know the value of those pregnant silences which come from having too much, not too little, to say. Even in detail this Mass, your Mass, will chime in with your mood, because for once you are keyed to the right pitch. But more noticeably holy Mass itself, in the whole shape and pattern of it, will be, for you, a Mass specially holy. It will be saying what you want to say to one another. For the Mass is a sacrifice; and when there is talk of sacrifice love is in its element.

There was a time when theologians held that destruction was the essence of sacrifice, and taxed their ingenuity in trying to prove that the Mass, somehow, involved a destruction of the sacred Elements. Today, they are for the most part content to claim that the essence of sacrifice is total offering. Such offering may—it did, on Calvary—involve destruction; but it needn't do so. The essence of sacrifice is rather total offering. We, in the Mass, make our imperfect offering of bread and wine, which becomes, by a miracle, the Body and Blood of Christ; at the same time, we offer ourselves, our souls and bodies, to be taken up into, made part of, his perfect sacrifice. And you two, in this Mass, your Mass, will present to him, at the Offertory, your love for one another; as perfect a thing as any human thing can be, yet, because it is human, still imperfect. You will ask him to take it up into, make it part of, his sacrifice; to supernaturalize it and eternalize it by that divine contact.

Your love for one another, a sacrifice—not in the sense that it means, for either of you, a loss of freedom, an abridgement of your personalities; but in the sense that it is the best thing in life you have to offer, and because it is the best, the most worthy of consecration. You offer it to God, to make what he wills of it; for better, for worse, for richer, for poorer, in sickness and in health, you make him the Master of your common destiny. We are forging a new link in human history, here in this chapel of our blessed Lady, which still stands, undeflected from its ancient purpose, among the ruins; it is impossible that our minds should not travel back to the past, and think of all those others who have plighted their vows on this very spot. From century to century the pattern of those human lives has been woven according to the designs of God's Providence; the same Providence watches, and will

Bridegroom and Bride

watch, over you. Only the consecration must be there; the undiminishing power of the Holy Mass must be allowed to overflow into your sacrifice. God bless you both, and fill your lives with that happiness which is the privilege of lives dedicated to him.

CHAPTER 10

The Nuptial Blessing

Increase and multiply. (Gen. 1:28 and 4:1)

THE CORE AND CENTRE OF THE MASS, CONSIDered as a sacrifice, is the recitation of our Lord's own prayer, the *Paternoster,* followed immediately by the *Libera nos,* and the breaking of the Sacred Host. You would have thought it impossible that the course of the Divine Mysteries should be interrupted just here. Nor (I think) is it ever so interrupted except, curiously, at the nuptial Mass. So hallowed, so privileged is this moment of dedication that for once the action of the Mass itself must be held up. And in the long form of blessing which is used on this occasion, there is one phrase which seems to emphasize the exceptional nature of it. "O God," says the priest, "through whom woman is joined to man, and this fellowship of theirs, instituted from the beginning of things, is endowed with that blessing which alone could not be revoked, either by the guilt of original sin, or by the sentence pronounced at the Deluge." Once when the world was created, and once again when it was preserved from universal destruction, the Divine Voice said: "Increase and multiply."

"That blessing which alone could not be revoked"—in pagan legend, when Pandora opened the box, one blessing alone was left to mankind, the blessing of hope. In the story of Genesis, when Eve forfeited her Paradise, one blessing alone, it seems, was left to mankind, the blessing of love. "They, hand in hand, with wandering steps and slow, Through Eden took their solitary way"—so Milton ends his epic; their world had crashed about them, but man and woman could still walk hand in hand—their marriage blessing was not revoked.

Treat the story of the Fall as you will, make what allowances you will for allegory, the central truth of it remains an ascertainable fact—man is born at war with his own nature; alone of God's creatures, he is confused, all the time, by a duality of purpose. "That I do is not something I wish to do, but something which I hate." Even when we are at our best—and how seldom we are at our best!—doing God's will presents itself, at the horizon of the mind, as something contrary to our inclinations. Because we are

Bridegroom and Bride

fallen creatures, there always seems to be a slight tug of reluctance which suggests that we are being false, now to the higher nature in us, now to the lower. But it is not so, when man and woman plight their marriage vows. Then, the primal blessing seems to light on us, uncancelled by the Fall. Then we come before God with such purity of intention that even at the very heart of the Mass the needs of bride and bridegroom do not seem out of place.

For a while, you two have escaped the sentry's watchfulness, and regained your Paradise. For indeed, Paradise is not a place from which we are exiled so much as a state from which we are alienated by the restless stirring of our own passions. To you, who can read the will of God in one another's eyes, unselfishness comes natural. Trust in God presents no difficulty to you; he has led you so wonderfully, and to so desirable a harbour. Faith costs no effort, because the immortal part in you has found its proper nourishment. Pride is in abeyance; you make the rare admission that life is treating you better than you deserve. Even that intimate disorder in our nature which allows the senses to dominate the soul is sublimated now. That you may never wholly awake from that vision, that the world may always have for you something of that bright colour which it has for you now, is the prayer your friends offer, envying you but not grudging you your happiness.

RONALD KNOX

Is the entertainment of such a hope presumptuous? Surely not. Ever since the curse pronounced upon our first parents was cancelled by the child-bearing of our Lady, the blessing pronounced upon man and wife has ceased to be the mysterious exception it once was. It has been caught up into the sacramental system of the Church, resupernaturalized by the grace of the new Covenant. "Behold," our Lord says, "I make all things new." And if the love which surrounds you and upholds you here and now, at the plighting of your troth, is of itself a human thing, subject like other human things to a law of diminution, will not the grace of this sacrament, an abiding influence, continually renew it; make it strike fresh roots; adapt it to the changing environment of your lives? You trust yourselves, you trust one another, to remain true while life lasts to the vows you have taken today. But, as Christian people, you can only trust yourselves, only trust one another, as enabled by God's grace to be, what your hearts tell you to be, always loyal, always unselfish, always considerate—lovers to the end. May he who has drawn you together with cords of love bind you together, in growing confidence, growing intimacy, and make your home a Nazareth, and your memory a blessing.

CHAPTER 11

The Christmas Present

*Then the kindness of God, our Saviour,
dawned on us; his great love for man.* (Titus 3:4)

WERE EVER TWO PEOPLE IN SUCH A HURRY TO GET married? Here is Christmas close upon us, and your friends have had to buy wedding presents just when they were in despair over their Christmas presents, and your wedding cake has been baking in the oven with Christmas cakes all about it! Well, since you would have a Christmas wedding, we will have a Christmas sermon for your wedding sermon. We will find a motto for your romance in this short sentence which occurs, so thrillingly, at the Epistle of the Aurora Mass on Christmas Day. St. Paul has been giving a terrible description of the world as it was in the days before Christ came; the great age of heathen civilization. "We, after all, were once like the rest of them…enslaved to a strange medley of desires and appetites, our lives full of meanness and envy, hateful, and hating one another. *Then* the kindness of God, our Saviour, dawned on us, his great love for man. He saved us; and it was not thanks to anything we had done for our own justification. In accordance with his own merciful design, he saved us."

Does it seem audacious to draw any comparison between the love of our Divine Redeemer, and this human love of ours, so cheapened in our minds by the sneers of the cynic, the misgivings of the psychologist? Then let me remind you that St. Paul himself is our authority for doing so; he has told us elsewhere that husbands must show love to their wives, as Christ showed love to the Church when he gave himself up on its behalf. Adam said of Eve, "Here at last is bone that comes from mine, flesh that comes from mine"; and St. Paul writes in the same way about Jesus Christ, the second Adam, "We are limbs of his body; flesh and bone, we belong to him." We understand something of what the Incarnation means, if we contemplate human love. We understand something of what human love means, if we contemplate the Incarnation.

The love which Jesus Christ showed in becoming Man was wholly unselfish; as the Apostle points out, it

Bridegroom and Bride

was not thanks to anything *we* had done. We were hateful, hating one another; there was nothing in us that could attract, if such a thing were possible, the Divine Love. *Propter nos homines*—that is the great mystery of the Incarnation; our Lord contrived to see something in us, although there was nothing to see. In every age, saints of his and good Christian people have been provoked by that challenge, and have given themselves up to the service of the despised, the neglected, the people from whom they could expect nothing in return. Is that sort of unselfishness in our minds, when we say that the love of man and woman is, and ought to be, modelled on the Incarnation?

Evidently not. A situation in which a man and woman married one another because each was sorry for the other, and for no other reason, might serve the turn of a modern novel—has done so, for all I know—but it would be a monstrosity in real life. God creates the love to reward the love; and you two, in the mutual understanding which you enjoy, find that perfect mirror which assures you, not only that you are loved, but that you are lovable. True, humility may protest, "This is beyond anything I have deserved; I shouldn't have thought there was anything in *me* anybody could have cared for." But in your hearts you know better; the mysterious bond which

RONALD KNOX

unites you is a two-way attraction, and it is something apart from your will; you could not escape from it even if, for some incredible reason, you wanted to. It costs you no effort, on either side, to love.

But then, this mysterious attraction of yours, so incalculable, part of you, yet not of your own making or of your own choosing—how can you be assured of its permanence? Might it not disappear as unaccountably as it came? Of itself, yes; but the sacrament you have received this afternoon has transformed it into something beyond itself. St. Paul tells us that "God does not repent of the gifts he makes, or of the calls he issues." That greatest of all gifts he made us, his Christmas present of Christ, is still ours, after so many centuries of unworthiness and ingratitude; even now, whoever calls on the name of the Lord will be saved. And the gift he has given you two this afternoon, is equally irrevocable; because he has called you to be husband and wife, he has given you the grace to live faithfully as husband and wife; and more than that, to live lovingly as bridegroom and bride; your romance is not to fade, as the things of time do; it is to live into eternity.

Only, here as elsewhere, grace cannot have its way with us unless we are prepared to co-operate with it. And you two will be wise enough to realize that this precious

Bridegroom and Bride

gift of love, now transformed into grace for you, is something that has to be lived up to; it mustn't be allowed to tarnish through your neglect. So it is well that in these first days of your married life you should have before you the example of the Christmas crib; St. Joseph with his unobtrusive protectiveness, and our Lady with her splendid capacity for making the most of things, and the Divine Infant above all with his kindness, his great love for man. May the peace and joy and humility of Bethlehem go with you, and make you look forward, with the breathless expectancy of Advent, to each anniversary of your wedding-day.

CHAPTER 12

Our Lady's Yes

Both the will to do it, and the accomplishment of that will, are something which God accomplishes in you, to carry out his loving purpose. (PHIL. 2:13)

I THINK THERE IS NO DAY IN ALL THE CALENDAR which could be a more auspicious wedding-day than this feast of our blessed Lady's Annunciation; that divine moment when all the future of unredeemed humanity waited on a woman's "Yes". So many artists have tried to picture her, with so many different models, in so many different styles, but always with the bowed head and the welcoming smile that proclaim her free consent. *Free* consent? Or are we tempted to doubt whether after all, at such a juncture, the human will could exercise its office? Pressure of grace within, in that soul where it was still Paradise; pressure of grace without, where that great angel, who is the strength of God, presumed instead of inviting her co-operation—was there room for that moment of decision in which the mind hesitates between Yes and No?...Well, we did not need to be told that the doctrine of grace is a mystery. Somehow, in that hour when she became part of the scheme of redemption, our Lady chose.

The divine mysteries, though they elude our grasp, are yet mirrored for us, as in a troubled surface, by the experiences of common life. There is a natural mystery about human free will, and it is forced on our attention whenever we assist at a wedding. "I will," "I will"—that is the hinge of the contract, that is the matter of the sacrament; no consent, no marriage. And is there not something almost suspicious, we begin to ask ourselves, about this echoed willingness? How can we be sure that there is a real act of choice, that the personality of bridegroom or bride has not cast a spell over bride or bridegroom, stampeded them into a false declaration? The answer to our scruples is that human love, like divine grace, does not abide our question; does not yield its secret to legal or logical analysis. Already, the two lovers have but one heart; to act, or to be acted upon, is all the same; a current of love passes between them, and the "I will" of either party is only that current of love bursting into flame.

Bridegroom and Bride

Have we spoken as if the love which unites the wills of man and woman were only the mirror of that love which unites man's will to the will of God? It is more; it is the echo, the continuation of it. Otherwise, how would it be possible for the bridegroom to say: "With my body I thee worship"? The use of that word "worship" in the wedding service—Catholic or Protestant, it is all one—has, before now, set us wondering. Are we using it in some obsolete sense, as when we describe a judge or a Lord Mayor as "His Worship"? Well, no doubt it has survived by accident, but it was a fortunate accident. I think you may say that Holy Church does permit the lover, in his moment of clear vision, to use an expression which borders on idolatry. For, after all, God's nature is not revealed to us only in his angels—in Gabriel, the Strength of God. It is revealed to us in all his works, even in our own fallen humanity. Strength, and courage, and beauty, and laughter, are a revelation of the divine in us; and when they are seen transfigured by a lover's eye they claim worship. Worship, the mood in which you are at once drawn towards the object of your desire, and at the same time repelled by a sense of unworthiness—"Who am I, that this should happen to me?" To love is to be very close to God.

And do not doubt, in this hour of fulfilment, that God is very close to you. That you should have met, that your lives should have imperceptibly grown together, was not an accident, any more than the angel's visit to Nazareth; it was part of God's plan for *you,* and for *you.* To be sure, every encounter in our lives is part of God's plan, but when he thus brings us together, man and woman, his Providence shows its hand; we look back at the stages of the journey we have travelled, and see it at work. We look back, and see how little all our projects and schemes had to do with it, how it all just happened, and we were powerless to prevent it; both the will to do it, and the accomplishment of that will, were something which God accomplished in us, to carry out his loving purpose—his, not ours. How hard it is, sometimes, to believe that the same set of events is Providential at once in this life and in that! Sometimes, but not here; God had his plan for each of you, and it was a plan for both. Either of you, like our Lady herself, was to be the accomplice of a divine purpose, integral, because he so willed it, to the sanctification of the other.

May our blessed Lady have you in her keeping; and always as this feast comes round, the feast of her Annunciation and of your wedding, may it bring back to you, year after year, the springtide of your romance.

CHAPTER 13

The Fruitful Vine

*Thy wife shall dwell in the innermost part of
thy house, like a fruitful vine.* (Ps. 127: 3)

I am the vine, you are its branches. (JOHN 15:5)

EASTER-TIDE IS RICH IN THE FEASTS OF MARTYRS; it was in spring, perhaps, that you got the best bookings for the amphitheatre. For all of them, the liturgy gives us a single, standardized Mass, a single, standardized Gospel—that of the true Vine. Not so much because that image appeals to us, at a time of year when we can almost watch the growth of every tendril on the trees; rather because this is Easter-tide, when we celebrate the risen life of Jesus Christ; the sap flowing in that Vine, the blood circulating in that Body, which is his Church. It was the strength of martyrs; among them, of our own

RONALD KNOX

St. George. It is the fertilizing source of all sacramental grace. And when our friends get married in Easter-tide, while we rejoice that nature itself should spread a carpet for them, we rejoice, more importantly, that the energy of our Lord's Resurrection should be thrusting forth, here among us, a new shoot of sacramental life.

The daughter of Caleb was given, for her wedding portion, both the upper and the lower springs. And if marriage takes its character both from nature and from grace, it is those higher springs that feed and invigorate it. The old Romans, by a natural metaphor, spoke of wedding the vine to the elm, because it clung close; we Christians look into the structure of the vine itself, and find there a more intimate symbol, not of mere closeness but of unity. St. Paul will have husbands love their wives on the same principle on which Christ loved his Church; he is not merely giving an illustration, he is pointing to human love as an offshoot of the divine. The love of a Christian man and woman for one another is but an expression of that charity which binds all Christians together; heartening to us others because it is felt and realized, because it is deep, because it is spontaneous.

"A fruitful vine upon the *walls* of thy house"; so ran the older translations, evoking the beautiful but inaccurate picture of some cottage nestling among the leaves.

Bridegroom and Bride

No, there is no attempt to work out the metaphor; the wife is represented as being always in the innermost part of the house; with a touch of Oriental possessiveness, it is indicated that woman's proper place is in the home. Forget that ungracious hint of the primitive; it remains true that there will be, there must be, an inner sanctuary in your wedded life which belongs only to you two; a sanctuary of mutual understanding. There will be touch of hand, turn of head, which you know how to interpret; there will be little jokes which nobody else shares, little allusions which nobody else quite sees the point of. And all that is symbolic of the fact that, at a much deeper level, you two will understand one another. Love is blind, they say; but that is at best only a half-truth; it overlooks only as the artist overlooks what is unessential; we others are distracted by detail, only love gives the full, rounded picture. "In the innermost part of thy house"—there will always, please God, be a threshold of intimacy between you which the world does not pass.

Only that is not quite the whole story. Forgive me if I seem to preach at you; it is your fault for asking me. There is a temptation, for man and woman newly wedded, to fence round this sacred intimacy of theirs unnecessarily, by keeping the rest of the world at arm's length. Oh, they are not conscious of it; but the weeks go on, and each is so utterly contented with the society of the other that nothing else seems to matter; invitations get refused, social activities neglected, public affairs seem remote and unreal. Two people living the best years of their life *only* for one another, and perhaps later on for their children; making hardly any contribution to the life of the neighbourhood, to the life of the parish, to the circle of their friends; impoverishing the world, impoverishing themselves, to keep their romance warm—as if it needed it!

"I am the Vine, you are its branches"—the grace which you have received this morning is nothing else than the love of Jesus Christ for his members, the love of his members for one another, polarized for you in this sacrament of love-giving. And it is not going to set you apart, shut you up in a world of make-believe, a little isolationist republic of two. It is the nature of love, the schoolmen tell us, to diffuse itself; and your love is meant to widen, not contract, your sympathy for others, make you more, not less apt to serve God in your generation. Every year, as the anniversary of our soldier-saint comes round, may you both thank God for what your wedding has meant to each, more strength, more courage, more discipline, to face the world with, learned, as it best should be, in the school of love. May the prayers of our blessed Lady go with you, and make your hearts always

Bridegroom and Bride

buoyant with the airs of spring, always clear and clean with the grace of Easter-tide.

CHAPTER 14

The Joyful Parting

A man is destined to leave his father and mother, and cling to his wife instead. (GEN. 2:24)

WHY IS IT THAT THE CHURCH FEASTS IN ASCENsion-tide? Why does she not proclaim a novena of solemn mourning, in which no joyful sound is heard, no voice of bridegroom and of bride, to commemorate those nine days of dereliction, when Jesus Christ had left our earth, and the Holy Spirit had not yet come down? In Ascension-tide we commemorate a parting, the breaking-up, so far as this life was concerned, of a circle of friends whom no common tie of loyalty had bound together, the separation of Jesus Christ from the Mother who so loved him, whom he so loved. But we do not mourn, because they did not mourn; they saw in that parting a glory and a fulfilment which outshone the sense of loss. They knew that he who was being taken from them had only been lent, not given to earth; he was going forward to achieve his human destiny, and should they, selfishly, hold him back?

Because of that, Ascension-tide shall be a time of feasting; the sounds of joy shall be heard in it, the voice of bridegroom and of bride. That old Hebrew tag is of happy omen to us this morning, as we come to witness two friends plighting their vows, and to wish them Godspeed. To wish them Godspeed, for in a sense we are parting from them; in a sense, every wedding is an unwedding. "A man is destined to leave his father and mother, and cling to his wife instead"—such was the divine decree, even in that happy world where man and woman had not yet left, to our sorrow, the Father who created them. The family was to be the cell by which the human race was to increase and multiply; when man and woman came together, a new home was in the making, and that meant, could only mean, the break-up of the old. Man and woman alike must leave father and mother; not in the sense of ceasing to love them, but in the sense that they were to find a new setting for their lives; the old circle would be impoverished, to enrich the new.

Forgive us, then, as you enter on this new-found happiness of yours, if there is something of a forced

Bridegroom and Bride

smile, something of a catch in the voice, when we congratulate you. We older people find it so hard to believe that our juniors have grown up, are of an age to marry and to live independent lives of their own. And even your contemporaries relinquish something when they see you plighted to one another; they think they will see less of you, you will live more for one another and less for them. Your wedding, for them, is an unwedding, but they will not grudge you the glory and the fulfilment of this hour, when you conspire, man and woman, to achieve your human destiny. Like the watchers at the Ascension, they will let their hearts go out with yours in rejoicing.

After all, it is only a sentimental kind of leave-taking on our side; we say goodbye not to you, but to something in you that was of its own nature impermanent—the irresponsible gaiety of first youth. And on your side, there is no leave-taking, no room for regrets. You are not relinquishing anything of the past; you are entering upon a natural heritage, as you set out together on the adventure of life; enlarging your own human stature, as you claim the privileges, and accept the responsibilities, of full citizenship. Just for the moment you feel as if you were withdrawing from the world, so as to live only for each other; you get away, with a sense of relief, from the congratulations and the photographers. But this ideal of cloistered

RONALD KNOX

retirement is only for the honeymoon; marriage does not withdraw us from the life we knew; it means that we wade deeper in the stream of it, take the strain of it more boldly than before.

When our Lord ascended into heaven, it was not so that he might keep clear of us men, forget our human needs, our human tragedies. He mounted up on high, St. Paul tells us, so that he might bring gifts to men, so that he might fill all creation with his presence; he was preparing the way for Pentecost. And he, who was our model while he lived on earth, was our model still in his manner of leaving it; when he grants us some great happiness, he means it to be shared with others. Every Christian home is a fresh cell split off from the parent stock, a new opportunity of impressing on the world the image of Christ. All that he has given you of strength and skill and charm and enterprise is to be a bond which binds you together, but it is to be something more; it is to be a contribution which you make, jointly now, to the building up of his kingdom among men. Your light is to shine before men not dimmed but reflected by the love that is your own secret.

I have called it an adventure, this act by which you have pledged yourselves in the sight of our ascended Master, each to the other, and both to him. Every important

Bridegroom and Bride

step we take here on earth is an adventure; "for better, for worse, for richer, for poorer, in sickness and in health"—the Church, with her brisk realism, does not allow us to forget it. Mounting up on high, our Lord gave gifts to men; may his gift to you be love, eager, considerate, understanding love, that can triumph over these accidents of mortality, and follow him at last, by his own path, to heaven.

CHAPTER 15

To Prepare a Home

I am going away to prepare a home for you. (JOHN 14:2)

WE ARE CELEBRATING AT THIS MOMENT TWO FEStivals which seem, at first sight, singularly ill matched. A festival of Britain, designed to re-kindle the love we feel for, the pride we take in, this parcel of earth which God has given us for our country. And the festival of our Lord's Ascension, which reminds us, year by year, that our true country lies not here, but in heaven. If you have got the whole Christian idea wrong, as many people have; if you persist in thinking that the supernatural is meant to cancel, to abrogate, to abolish the natural—then indeed we are trying to play two tunes at once. We are reminding ourselves of our British citizenship just when we ought to be reminding ourselves that our citizenship is in heaven.

RONALD KNOX

But it is not so; the natural and the supernatural do not clash, do not conflict; they supplement one another. The love which we bear for our earthly country is a sacrament, the sacramental expression of the love which we bear, as Christians, for a heavenly country which is to be ours hereafter. That imperfect harmony which exists between us as fellow citizens helps us to form some idea of the perfect harmony which exists in heaven. That perfect harmony which exists in heaven is the model by which we, fellow citizens, must strive to live on earth. Type and antitype implement one another.

Do not be surprised, then, do not be impatient with me, if I quote those words of our Lord, "I am going away to prepare a home for you"—a home in heaven, just when you two are preparing to set up a home on earth. Marriages are out of place during Lent, but not in Ascension-tide, although in Ascension-tide our Lord seems to be parting from us, and separation rather than union is uppermost in our thoughts. But you see, he is not really parting from us. He is going away to make a home for us, that is all. St. Paul loves to describe the Church as the Bride of Christ; and when, in Ascension-tide, he leaves us for a little, it is only because he, the Bridegroom, wants to get the home ready for himself and his Church. There could be no more auspicious moment, if you come to think of it, for getting married.

Bridegroom and Bride

For you, then, today's event is, not in lover's language but in cold theological fact, a foretaste of heaven. It is by entering, as best we may, into the secret of your happiness that we others try to imagine what heaven is like. We have lived too long, and forgotten the greater emotions; we are tempted to think of heaven as if it were a mere rest from striving, a mere release from our worries, and uncertainties. We want to see it in the light of your triumphant experience as the thing it is—the time of waiting over, the troth kept, the reward claimed, not less confidently because it was won beyond all our deserving. Heaven as achievement, heaven as new life, heaven as perfect union—all those half-forgotten ideals we read in your happiness today.

For us, then, to see heaven as earth's counterpart; for you to understand and interpret today's adventure by reading it in the light of heaven. Heaven is enduring love, love that endures without effort; heaven is a happiness into which the thought of self does not enter; heaven is all giving, and giving without cost. Of all that, we can find no nearer image on earth than the love of man and woman. Only, because it is of earth, that image remains imperfect. Earthly love cannot survive the stress of everyday living without the need of sacrifices on both sides; sacrifices which at first are hardly felt, but grow more conscious and more difficult as the years go by. For this reason, you come here to ask for the grace of Christ's sacrament of matrimony; that he, who has gone to prepare a home for us in heaven, may prepare a home for you on earth.

When our Lord went back to make a home for us in heaven, he must have watched the landscape receding from his view, all those familiar scenes which had been the context of his life as Man. Far below him lay Nazareth, where his presence had perfected the happiness of a perfect human home; and surely his blessing rested on it, as he took his farewell of earth. He remembered all those little events of his boyhood which come out in his parables; his Mother putting leaven in the dough, and the day when the silver coin was lost, and the friend who came round late at night asking for a loaf of bread. And I like to think that this parting benediction of his was meant for every Christian home, in which he and his Blessed Mother and St. Joseph would be remembered; all the absurd little incidents of everyday life should be hallowed by his presence, as they were in the home at Nazareth, and whenever difficulties or disagreements arose, he would be there to put everything right. May that blessing rest upon you, and upon the home which he is preparing for you; may the human love you feel for one another

Bridegroom and Bride

be enriched and deepened and controlled by that current of divine love which flows to us through the sacraments from the life of God himself; and may that same love prepare for both of you, at last, a home in heaven.

CHAPTER 16

Veni, Sancte Spiritus

> *North wind, awake, wind of the south, awake
> and come: blow through this garden of mine,
> and set its fragrance all astir.* (CANT. 4:16)

OWING TO A FOOLISH PAGAN SUPERSTITION, which has died harder than any other, people seldom get married in May. And May is the month of Pentecost; the feast falls in that month more than twice as often as in June. Very few people, consequently, claim the privilege you have claimed today, of entering upon your married life under the most appropriate auspices that could be imagined, in the name and power of the Holy Spirit.

The Holy Spirit is himself that bond of love which unites and completes the Godhead. And of that divine love earthly love must needs be the reflection. We shrink from the analogy; memories of an Italian picture bid us think of sacred and profane love as two things essentially contrasted. But, if language is to have any meaning, there must be some common element in two things which are called by the same name; and if our theology is to make sense, earthly love can only be some echo of, some approximation to, the divine. We have a rooted tendency, coming down to us from the Reformation, to keep the natural and the supernatural worlds apart. The natural world belongs to the scientists, with their microscopes, to the historians with their documents; the world of grace is something loosely tacked on to, jealously screened off from, the world of our experience. The Holy Spirit—we do not imagine him as playing any part in the history of the universe until he came down on the day of Pentecost. That is heresy; the *Credo* assures us that he spoke by the prophets. But was that all—is it only in a strictly religious context that we can trace his influence?

The men of the Middle Ages, with their *naïf* but better integrated view of life, found a more satisfactory place for the action of the Holy Spirit in their world-picture. Had not the Spirit of God brooded over the waters when creation began? Had not the wise man told us that the spirit of the Lord fills the whole world? They would address him as the Love that "all things fillest, all things lovest, planets guidest, heaven movest," as the ultimate

Bridegroom and Bride

source of all the stir and motion that goes on around us. Love, somehow, must be the secret of this world, as of the next. That broad, mystical sweep of medieval thought is something we need not pin down with theological definitions; but we cannot lose sight of it if we are to attempt any understanding of what God is, and how the world is his shadow.

Grace does not abolish or contradict the strivings of nature; it perfects and hallows them. And the Sacrament of Matrimony is a gracious reminder of that truth. The love of man and woman, even if you take it in the raw, is something which transcends the common possibilities of human nature, pushes through that veil of selfishness in which human nature, since we lost Paradise, is fatally enwrapped. "Love," says the *Imitation of Christ*, "makes every burden light to carry, bears with equanimity the unequal lot; burden is no burden that is so shouldered, and the bitterest cup becomes sweet and pleasant to the taste." It is to divine love that the passage refers; but human love has, in our common experience, the same quality. And what grace does in this sacrament is to supernaturalize, if the paradox may be excused, something which is already supernatural in its essence and in its mode of expression. The Holy Spirit, like the winds invoked by the bridegroom in the

RONALD KNOX

Canticles, seems only to bring out the fragrance of a gift that is already divine.

But there is more than that. Our blessed Lord, when he promised the coming of the Holy Spirit, to befriend the Apostles in his own stead, made it clear that this was to be an *abiding* presence; "he will be continually at your side, nay, he will be in you." It was only for such a short time that Incarnate God had pitched his tent among us—this new manifestation of the Godhead should be for all time. An abiding presence; we are men, and seven times pass over us; the joys of earth dazzle us for a moment, then slip through our fingers and are gone. This new-found happiness of yours is something almost terrifying; it is so delicate a thing that you feel it must needs be fragile—you are like children who want to hand over some precious gift to their mother for fear they should lose it. And it is a true instinct of yours that bids you bring it here and entrust it to the Church for safe-keeping. So your human love becomes part of that divine love which the presence of the Holy Spirit evokes in our hearts. *Sine tuo numine nihil est in homine, nihil est innoxium*—even the purest and the most gracious of God's gifts, in this imperfect world, carry within them the seeds of decay, until the touch of the supernatural elevates and transmutes them.

Bridegroom and Bride

May the home which the plighting of your vows today inaugurates be a home in which he, the Spirit of truth, is ever a welcome guest, *in labore requies, in aestu temperies, in fletu solatium,* your repose, your refreshment, your consolation. And may our blessed Lady look kindly on two children of hers, married in May, and keep you always under her protection.

CHAPTER 17

The Easy Yoke

Take my yoke upon you and learn of me; I am gentle and humble of heart. (Matt. 11:29)

THERE IS A CERTAIN VALVE IN THE HUMAN BODY which is of the utmost importance to us, because it controls the circulation of the blood, but (so the men of science tell us) has no particular connection with the life of the mind. Yet from the earliest times mankind has been content to regard it as the seat of our conscious life. Not of the emotions merely; in the Bible, "heart" nearly always means intellect; when you want a pupil to pay attention, you say: "My son, give me thy heart," and when our blessed Lady is puzzled by the mystery of her Divine motherhood, it is in her heart that she ponders over it. Only in the Middle Ages, I think, was the heart identified as specially the seat of the emotions, only then did it become a symbol to lovers; and the contrast we make nowadays between head and heart, ascribing our thoughts to the one and our feelings to the other, is more modern still.

In the same way, devotion to the Sacred Heart of our Lord Jesus Christ is properly, was originally, nothing more or less than a devotion to the Sacred Manhood. But because St. Margaret Mary told us about her visions, told us how our blessed Lord laid bare his bosom to her, and bade her pity the heart that loved so much, and was loved so little in return, what we venerate chiefly in these days of June is the love, the divine-human love, which brought him down from heaven and persuaded him to give himself so freely. We have been living so much in an atmosphere of theological mystery, from Easter to the Ascension, from the Ascension to Pentecost, and then the Trinity and the Real Presence on the top of that; now at last, when we get to the feast of the Sacred Heart, we feel it is something we can understand. We can't really; it's the hardest mystery of the lot; why did our Lord love us? How could he love us? But we think we can understand it, and we feel it to be the greatest romance of all time—God coming down from heaven *propter nos homines,* for love of us men, and the Church as the Bride of Christ which he loved and gave himself for it, so as to

Bridegroom and Bride

win it for himself. Love comes into its own, in these June days.

Our Lord wants this generosity of his to be infectious. "If I have washed your feet, I who am the Master and the Lord, you in your turn ought to wash one another's feet." And again, "Take my yoke upon you and learn from me, I am gentle and humble of heart." My yoke, not simply the yoke which I impose on you; the yoke which I, too, have taken on myself, the yoke I share with you. That is for all of us, but more especially he looks to find it when man and woman come before him to receive the Sacrament of Matrimony. For this sacrament is, in a special sense, the mirror of his own love; St. Paul has told us about it. "You who are husbands must show love to your wives, as Christ showed love to the Church when he gave himself up on its behalf." Husband and wife are to give themselves up, Christ-fashion, to each other.

Marriage is a yoke. The Latin language, with its strong sense of realities, gives husband and wife the name of yoke-fellows. And those who would bear the yoke together must keep in step—instinctively or by an effort. So instinctively do you march together as you set out on your journey, that you can hardly imagine why the subject should be mentioned; could it ever gall, such a yoke as yours? It will not gall, if you bear it Christ-fashion; his yoke is easy, and his burden is light, but only on condition that we learn from him the secret of shouldering it. It is in the Sacred Heart that we shall find heart's ease.

"I am gentle and humble of heart"—no need to discuss the words in detail. Words change their overtones, when they are translated from one language into another, change their emphasis, when they are transported from one century into another. We shall form a just appreciation of them, not by turning up the Greek lexicon, but by studying the life of Jesus Christ. How perfectly he keeps step, Godhead mated with Manhood! How patient he is with slow wits, how ready to consider every appeal, to answer the most irrelevant questions; how constantly at everybody's disposal, how gentle in drawing people out, leading people on! It is the courtesy, the considerateness of Jesus Christ that most of us lack, all of us need. To see everything from the other person's point of view; what will be the effect of a casual criticism, whether such and such a proposal is being welcomed, or merely complied with; to be alert, receptive, ready with your enthusiasms—how little all that seems, how much it means! And not least in marriage. Forgive us, if these seem to be petty and niggling wishes from your well-wishers, to speed you on your way. The secret behind it all is love; that the love with which you are now pledging yourselves to the

Bridegroom and Bride

yoke may grow ever deeper and truer, unfading with the years, undimmed by experience, undaunted by difficulties, *that* is the prayer we make for you. And making it, we leave it where the fountain and the furnace of all love is, in the keeping of the Sacred Heart.

CHAPTER 18

Nihil Fortius Amore

Death itself is not so strong as love. (Cant. 8:6)

IF WE READ THE SONG OF SONGS AS A CONTINUOUS drama, the last chapter of it represents a scene of strong human interest. Country lover and country girl, reunited at last, walk together down the village street, marked by everybody, and longing to be alone. In the first verse, she wishes that she were his sister, and that they could go out together without people turning to look at them. And in the last two verses he makes the same complaint: "Where is thy love of retired garden walks? All the country-side is listening to thee. Give me but the word to come away, thy bridegroom, with thee; hasten away, like gazelle or fawn that spurns the scented hillside under foot." She so loth to be watched, he so loth to be overheard; could there be a more natural picture of two village lovers?

RONALD KNOX

You and I, who have come to witness this ceremony—can we acquit ourselves of a failure in tact? Bride and bridegroom are exchanging their whispered vows in the sight of God; must they be embarrassed by a crowd of intruders, looking, listening? Let us hasten to make our excuses. We come as their fellow-citizens, to witness the ratifying of a solemn contract. We come as their fellow-Christians, to invite by our prayers that great outpouring of grace which an occasion like this so urgently needs, so confidently claims.

Every marriage is an event in human history; in the tapestry which Divine Providence weaves out of our lives, love of man for woman and love of woman for man are warp and woof. When the paths of man and woman meet, there is an adventure; an adventure upon which the survival of our race depends. Two stars have met in conjunction; or, to speak more literally and more Christianly, two angel guardians are to be engaged, henceforward, in a common task of tutelage. A new home is being set up, a new unit in world-affairs. For it is the family, not the parish or the nation, that is the real unit in world-affairs. A man fights, ultimately, in defence of his own backyard; a woman saves to keep her own children from starving. Every wedding is a society wedding; it is on the well-being of the family that society depends.

Bridegroom and Bride

We are here, then, as their fellow-citizens, to assure ourselves that bride and bridegroom are laying well and truly the foundations of a new home; that is, in perfect mutual trust, which makes it seem a little thing to vow life-long fidelity. We are here, far more importantly, as their fellow-Christians, to ask that this love of theirs, so bright with the ardour of youth, may glow with the radiance of eternity. To them it seems unalterably firm already, the chain of their affections; they must forgive us if we pronounce natural love an unsafe anchorage in a world so fugitive. We would take those cords of Adam which already bind them, and wrap them round, wrap them round, with the strands of that heavenly love which alone is imperishable. We would have their memories of the event we are witnessing today interwoven with the whole of their sacramental life, so that they never see an altar again without being reminded of *this* altar; we would have the promises made in our presence here crystallized as part of their religion. Love strong as death.

When we speak of fidelity to Christian marriage vows, we do not use that word in a merely legal sense, as implying that the bond here welded will remain for ever unbroken. God forbid we should take so low a view of what matrimony and the grace of matrimony are intended to be. If you were souls entering religion, we should not be wishing you a life-time of unwilling imprisonment within the walls of your institute; we should be wishing you unclouded faith in the vocation to which God had called you, long days of happy service, and a full measure of the Divine consolation when dark times came. So it is with matrimony; the prayer we offer is that neither of you should know what it is to feel any transient regret over the choice you made; that your lives should be a long conspiracy of devoted partnership; that whatever unkindness fortune may have in store for you, it should seem a light matter, borne in such companionship. We are wishing you, what only God's grace can give you, a life-long romance.

With that in mind, we do not scruple to leave you under the patronage of today's saint, St. Mary Magdalen; one who loved so well that the memory of her love has obliterated, in God's mind and man's, the memory of her sins. Love was hers as strong as death; stronger than death, or why would she alone persevere in the search of her Master, dead or alive? Love was not content to direct her will, it dominated her feelings; may the love you feel for one another be there still, and be felt still, until death parts you for a little. And may our blessed Lady and St. Joseph be, for you and for all of us, the patrons and the models of the Christian home.

CHAPTER 19

St. Mary on the Quay

And so we knelt down on the beach to pray. (ACTS 21:5)

HOW VERY FEW CHURCHES ARE BEAUTIFULLY named! As a rule, nowadays, we invoke a whole litany of saints for the christening of a church, and set it down in one of our ill-sounding suburbs, and the result is some such mouthful as "St. Thérèse of Lisieux and the English Martyrs, Lower Puddlington." What a relief to the ear when you come across some title which has the charm of simplicity; when you are told: "The wedding service was at St. Mary's on the Quay." Because you have turned your backs, you two, on the fashionable London centres where one bridal procession treads on the heels of the last, and have preferred to plight your vows in this ancient city, the church in which you were married will have a special meaning for you—*your* church; and the name of it will

RONALD KNOX

be musical to you beyond all others; "St. Mary's on the Quay."

Forgive me, then, if, on the eve of her great feast, in a year when we are encouraged to hold her specially remembered, in a church dedicated, so unobtrusively, to her, I turn your thoughts towards the blessed Mother of Christ—should not such a conjunction have an auspicious influence on the horoscope of your lives? It is a natural metaphor, when we compare any great undertaking, any fresh departure, to a voyage by sea. And you, who are embarking on the familiar but inexhaustible adventure of marriage, are like seafarers impatient to be gone, while their friends crowd round and importune them with fond messages, with homely, practical advice. So, in the Acts of the Apostles, we read that St. Paul's friends at Tyre crowded round him, as he went up to Jerusalem: "All of them, with their wives and children, escorted us until we were out of the city; and so we knelt down on the beach to pray." Let that gracious picture be in our minds, as we bid you Godspeed on the journey of a life-time. And with us— in fact or in fancy, it does not matter—stands the Mother of Christ, in her going-away dress, all ready for tomorrow; waves her good wishes to you; St. Mary on the Quay.

What are the parting messages she would leave with you, amid the bustle and confusion of your sailing? Let

Bridegroom and Bride

us go to the Gospels, and read there her recipe for making a success of life. We don't need to go beyond the first chapter of St. Luke; all the rest of her history follows automatically, you might almost say, from her attitude at the Annunciation. "Behold, the handmaid of the Lord; let it be unto me according to thy word"—we have all been surprised, before now, at the curiously detached way in which she says it. She has just been given her sailing orders for the most momentous life-voyage of all time; she is to be the Ark in which the Salvation of the world is to ride on the flood of human wickedness. And she accepts them with a kind of naval promptitude; "let it be unto me according to thy word"—that is all. But, believe me, it is everything.

Let it not be thought that because her destiny was so infinitely higher than yours or mine, your attitude and mine ought to be different from hers. Every wedding announcement in the newspapers is a kind of annunciation; it is, for two human souls, their great moment, the opportunity of a life-time. Providence has been at work, in the humblest as in the greatest of human fortunes; the unpredictable attraction which has brought two souls together and knitted them together is a sort of splendid coincidence which betrays the divine purpose. So far, everything has been done for them; they themselves could not tell you how it has happened, why they, who might have been ships that pass in the night, find themselves travelling in convoy. But now it is their turn to take a hand and co-operate; they accept the situation, and the echoes of Nazareth's *Fiat mihi* tremble in the words, "I will."

Oh, this is an ungracious moment to remind you of it, but the voyage of life is not all plain sailing; unexplored tests await you beyond the sheltered waters of your honeymoon. He travels the fastest, they say, who travels alone; and you two, each of you, have accepted a destiny which means making a success of two lives, instead of one. If you would thrive in that adventure, there is no attitude possible except to welcome God's will, as the Mother of Christ did at the Annunciation, when she accepted Bethlehem and Calvary both in one. And it must be a joint declaration: "Behold, the servant and the handmaid of the Lord; let it be to *us* according to thy word." We, who have come here to pray for God's blessing on your marriage, wish you long life, and prosperity, and if it be his will, the joys of parenthood. But above all we wish for you, in full measure, the grace of this sacrament, to keep you true to one another, each the comfort and support of the other, in all the vicissitudes of fortune; may there be no joy and no sorrow which does not draw

Bridegroom and Bride

you closer together. And when the journey is over, may she, who gives you your send-off today, be waiting there to welcome you; St. Mary on the Quay.

CHAPTER 20

On the Palm of My Hands

*Behold, I have graven thee on
the palms of my hands.* (Isa. 49:16)

WE ARE MEN, AND OUR JOURNEY THROUGH LIFE IS a short one; yet we must always be diversifying it with landmarks, as if we feared that the days would run by too monotonously. The year's course shall be studded for us, here and there, by the associations of the past; a birthday, a wedding-day, somebody's anniversary, shall be a focus for memory. Each of us has his own calendar; and this runs side by side with the Church's calendar, intersecting it, as road and river intersect in the changing landscape that unfolds itself to the traveller's eye. Such and such an event in my life fell upon such a feast-day—now we derive some happy omen from it, now we accept it with a sense of delicious incongruity. How will it be with you two, wedded on the day on which our Lord granted the marks of his Passion to St. Francis? The Italian landscape so familiar to both of you; and yet, when you come across the picture of Francis kneeling in prayer on the chilly slopes of La Verna, it will speak to you, not of Italy, but of Somersetshire orchards, and the sluggish channels of Sedgemoor!

You will not be sorry, I think, to have embarked on life's adventure under such patronage. For the granting of the Stigmata surely meant, in the inner life of St. Francis, that decisive moment which we call the Spiritual Marriage. We are talking, when we use such language, about things of which we know nothing; the saints themselves are hard put to it when they try to stammer out to us the breathless fragments of their experience. But there comes a moment, it seems, in the long romance between our blessed Lord and the soul which has tried to give up a whole life to him, when the sacrifice is made absolute, when the compact is irrevocably sealed—so far at least as anything in this world of our probation can be called irrevocable. Our Lord says to the faithful soul, in the words he used to Isaiah, "I have graven thee on the palms of my hands"; the record is indelible—whatever surprises await us on the Day of Judgement, *cum vix justus sit securus*, that name will be found written in the Book of Life. And,

Bridegroom and Bride

in return—what should our Lord do but take his lover by the hand and stamp the record there no less indelibly? The saint, too, who has been through that experience can say: "I have graven thee on the palms of my hands"; and Francis could show the sign-manual of it for all the world to see.

May this sacrament, which you are administering to one another today, convey to both of you that unalterable fidelity which the gift of the Stigmata betokened. To both of you; when we give ourselves to God we establish, in cold theological fact, no claim on him; we are only giving him what is his already, we are only performing our bare duty as his creatures. But God is faithful—that is the *leitmotiv* of all the Old Testament; not bound to us by justice, he is bound to us by that fidelity which is a part of his own nature. He has promised to reward us, and that promise is as certain a pledge as any his justice could give us. When he gave St. Francis the Stigmata, our Lord was not simply putting a brand on him, as the shepherd brands his sheep, simply saying: "This is mine." He was saying, like the bride in the Canticles, "He is mine, and I am his." The wounds on the hands of Francis were only the counterpart, only the image, of that invisible transaction by which Francis was graven on the hands of Christ.

RONALD KNOX

And so it is with bride and bridegroom. When the man puts a ring on the woman's finger, an uninstructed bystander might easily be mistaken. He might suppose that the ring was a symbol of bondage, like the ring round the bird's talon that proclaims, "This is mine." It is not like that; the ring is the symbol of a mutual compact, entrusted to the woman only because women are so much better at keeping things than men. The protestation it makes is not: "This person belongs to me," but: "I belong to this person." The ring is not a symbol of captivity; rather of unbroken unity and unending changelessness; the perfect round.

If we ask why St. Francis is such a popular favourite among the saints, even outside the Church, the answer must be, I think, that he is a saint of the sunlight. He does not shut himself up in a cloister to get away from God's creatures; he goes out into the open air, and accepts God's creatures as they come. He is so gay, so carefree; he does not spend all his time trying to make himself unhappy; he is the saint of the Christmas Crib. All that; and yet he carried about with him on hands and feet the image, not of Christ glorified but of Christ crucified; there was suffering in Francis' life, as there must be suffering in the lives of all saints, and of all men. So, during the wedding service, when nobody is looking, the priest gets hold of

Bridegroom and Bride

the ring and traces over it the sign of the cross. Over that symbol of perfect happiness, the Church bids him trace the sign of sacrifice. Always she sees things steadily, as they are, not through a mist of sentiment; and she knows that the wedding-service is not just the prelude to a honeymoon—it is the prelude to the whole of marriage.

You have undertaken to live a shared life. It will have its crosses, great or small; each of you will be blessed in having another to bear them as well, blessed still more in having another person's crosses to bear. Each will have sacrifices to make for the other; both, perhaps, will have sacrifices to make for other lives than your own. That you may carry your crosses as gaily as Francis carried his, that you may enjoy your happiness with the simplicity with which Francis enjoyed his, is the blessing your friends wish you on this joyful and sorrowful feast. May his prayers, and the prayers of our blessed Lady and St. Joseph, win you a joyful home on earth, and a joyful home-coming in heaven.

CHAPTER 21

His Own Sheep

He calls by name the sheep which belong to him, and leads them out with him. (JOHN 10:3)

"ONE WEDDING," YOU WILL HEAR PEOPLE SAY, "IS very much like another." In a sense, that observation is true; in another sense, profoundly untrue. Superficially, we all know how true it is; such pains taken to make this wedding rather different; some hint, at least, of originality about the flowers, about the bridesmaids' dresses, about the hymns, even about the sermon. And yet, when you say you met somebody the other day at a wedding, how hard to remember whose wedding! When you describe how beautifully the church was decorated, how hard to remember what church! Even at a more philosophical level, how can one wedding be different from the next? It is the same old story; two human beings attracted to one another, and uniting to set up a home; nature's way of seeing to it that the race does not die out. Births, marriages and deaths—so human history unfolds itself, in monotonous routine.

But, for you two, it is different; this is like no other wedding you have ever been to. The familiar words of the service—at any other wedding, you could have prompted bride and bridegroom from your own memory; now, you have to repeat them stammeringly after the priest as if they were a child's lesson; the mind is too confused to act as interpreter between heart and lips. The music you planned so carefully goes, for you, unheard; or at best serves as a kind of background to that inner music which you only can hear. Your friends, the familiar friends whom you invited to share your happiness, have disappeared; all around you is a sea of faces, quite kind, quite encouraging, but somehow all strangers to you. Even the scent of the flowers bewilders you, you cannot put a name to them; you feel (like George Fox), "Now I was come up into the Paradise of God; all things were new, and all the creation gave another smell unto me than before, beyond what words can utter."

Which point of view is the true one? The picture seen from the outside, by the casual onlooker, or the picture seen from the inside, by the two people principally

Bridegroom and Bride

concerned? At a hundred chance encounters, life confronts us with the same familiar problem, and always the answer is the same; things are not as you see them nor as we see them but as God sees them. And how does God see it? Does this wedding look to him just the same as any other wedding, or quite different from every other wedding? Why, both at once.

In a sense, all we have done this morning is to sew one more stitch into the great pattern of history. Two families intermarry, and with that a thousand modifications of physique, a thousand tricks of temperament, derived from long-forgotten ancestries, beyond all the calculations of the biologists flow together into the same stream, ready to repeat themselves in an indefinite series. Just like any other wedding, just one more rearrangement of human destinies, one more flick of the Potter's hand, so skilful, so unchanging.

And yet, because man is soul as well as body, and every soul is an unique creation, this wedding is different from every other wedding in God's eyes; in his eyes who made all things, and does not lose interest in anything he has made. For that reason, when he came to earth, he told us that he knows his own sheep by name. A flock of sheep, so indistinguishable to us, but to the shepherd each one is different. And to him, today's bridegroom and bride are not simply bridegroom and bride, but Francis and Therese. Names, we may be sure, very dear to him; they have associations of their own. But the Therese who takes this Francis, the Francis who takes this Therese, are different from all the others; he, the Good Shepherd, knows them by name; and he has made them for one another. The old heathens used to represent the God of Love as blind; the God of Love whom we Christians know sees everything, sees into everyone, and he, the perfect Match-maker, has made this match.

Because we know that each of you is personally dear to him, because we believe that it is he who made your paths cross, and drew you together, we send you out confidently into a world so full of uncertainties as this. May the prayers of our blessed Lady and St. Joseph go with you on your journey, may they win for each of you, win for both of you, the graces you need for the life you are to live together, and bid you rejoice at last because your names are written in heaven.

CHAPTER 22

Leading-Strings of Love

*Sons of Adam, they should be drawn with
leading-strings of love.* (HOS. 11:4)

HOW FOND THE HEBREW PROPHETS ARE OF DEscribing the early history of their nation—the escape from Egypt, the wanderings in the desert, the conquest of Chanaan—in terms of a romance! A honeymoon period, so it seemed to the men of a later time, when they followed, at every turn of their fortunes, a divine, a visible leadership; when each experience of theirs, each contact with their fellow men, formed part of their education, schooled them to trust God more, to cast off the slough of heathendom.

The Providence of God—hard to believe it, yet impossible to disbelieve it—is shaping, all the while, the destinies of this or that nation, this or that soul. No

RONALD KNOX

experience we pass through but leaves some dent on our character; still more noticeably, the *people* we associate with become, unconsciously, our schoolmasters, and perhaps our destiny. Look back, and remember how you caught from A. your tricks of handwriting; how your admiration for such-and-such an author was learned from B.; how C.'s influence came between you and what seemed the habit of a life-time. The same power that moves the heavenly bodies by attraction and repulsion moves, by attraction and repulsion, our earthly bodies, and with them our immortal souls. More than all else, likings and dislikings determine the brief orbit of human life.

A marriage, the intersection of two human destinies, is a planetary conjunction which sets us all star-gazing. "Where did they meet?" we ask commonly enough, and the question is less inept than it sounds. The hand of God, "accident," as we foolishly call it, must play its part first in bringing two human fates together; each entry in the marriage register means one moment of time eagerly remembered, one spot of ground for ever consecrated. This was no casual meeting, however much it might seem so; among all the myriad contacts of *your* life-time and *yours,* this one caught fire, took wing, became fruitful. Two earthly bodies were attracted, either to other—bodies, for we men are body and soul sacramentally united;

Bridegroom and Bride

no room here for the shallow religiosity which would treat the outward part of us as something meaningless, negligible. And, through the windows of the body, soul looked out to soul. The Providence that plots out all our journeyings was drawing them, not, this time, at haphazard, but with leading-strings of love.

To each of you, then, because your paths have met, we wish happiness. To each of you, or rather to both of you, because henceforward there is no *each*, only *both*; you can have no happiness now except what is shared between you. We wish you prosperity and health, but more than these, the quality which can dispose of, and dispense with, either of these—love sharpened to the point of unselfishness. This it was, above all, God meant to teach you, when he drew you to one another and drew you to himself with those leading-strings of love—that we become ourselves only when we pass out of ourselves, find happiness only when the happiness we aim at, and strive for, is not ours. The lesson of a lifetime; and it comes so easily to you now!

Do not be angry with us, do not think us cynical, if we look about us to find some means of making it permanent, that touching gesture of mutual self-giving which you showed us, with joined hands, just now. Adam's sons and Eve's daughters, we are marred in the making, and there is no Paradise we do not know how to lose. Do not think Mother Church importunate, if she hurries up, at such a moment, with the offer of sacramental grace, to keep you true to one another, through life and beyond. It is not a substitute for love she offers; grace does not destroy nature, only brings it to perfection. The influence of the sacrament is not, believe me, to canalize the impetuous course of your love; rather, it will feed at deeper springs. It will feed from that living current of charity which brought our Lord Jesus Christ down to earth, to win the Church for his bride, and draw all the sons of Adam back to him with leading-strings of love.

May the prayers of our blessed Lady and St. Joseph go with you on your journey, drawing the clasp of your hands ever closer, and winning abundantly God's blessing on your wedded life.

CHAPTER 23

The True Vision

Blessed are the eyes that see what you see. (LUKE 10:23)

WHY IS IT THAT SO MANY OF US WANT TO CRY when we go to weddings? I think, because man and woman in love bring back to us some flavour of primal innocence. The cherubs hold up their flaming swords, and we catch some glimpse, if only for a moment, of the Paradise we have lost.

To be worldly-wise is the boast of our generation. There is no nonsense about us; we look things squarely in the face; we have seen through the sham sentiment, the polite conventions of yesterday…If that is all the wedding garment you bring to church with you, rest assured that you will find here plenty of material for cynicism. A man and a woman, you exclaim, who look at one another with bewitched eyes, and see qualities, excellences which are not there! This is not really the most remarkable man in the world, nor this the most remarkable woman in the world; it is only that they see one another through rose-coloured spectacles. A fortunate illusion makes either of them blind to the other's faults; that is all.

Such a judgement is wrong; is exquisitely wrong. The fact is that we need these rose-coloured spectacles of yours, all of us, to correct our own jaundiced outlook, fallen creatures in a fallen world. We look round at our fellow men and women, and can see nothing but their faults; the closer we are brought to them, the longer our intimacy with them, the more we become critical of them. They are hidden, for us others, behind the coating of dust that is left over from Eve's transgression, Adam's transgression; if only we had the magic of your clear vision, to pierce through that and see men and women as they really are, splendid and lovable! It is given to you, at this moment, to see human nature as God sees it, to love it as God loves it.

Nor is this love of yours selfishly limited, although (it may be) you have eyes only for one another. Bride and bridegroom want everybody else to be as happy as themselves; that is why they summon us to be with them, that is why they feast us. Did not our Lord compare the calling-in of the Gentiles to a wedding feast? When you are

Bridegroom and Bride

getting married, the love that is so specialized broadens out into a kind of general benevolence; the cabmen who drive you to church seem splendid people, the registrar waiting in the sacristy becomes a recording angel with a pen of gold. Seeing, just for this once, the goodness and the beauty of human nature, you are half in love with all mankind. Dare we say it? It is given to you to see human nature as God sees it, mirrored in the Incarnation of his Son.

Lovers, in that season of their love's flowering, see truly where we others see amiss. More fortunate still, they react right to a situation, as if they had the instinct of unfallen creatures. Which of us has ever known what it is, to worship? How clumsily we throw ourselves into attitudes, how woodenly we repeat formulas, trying to persuade ourselves that we are worshipping God! But these know just what it is; "with my body I thee worship"—know what it is to feel awe and reverence before something too sacred to admit of approach, yet infinitely desirable; to be attracted and repelled both at once; to give themselves with whole-hearted surrender, to want to belong to each other. That attitude which we others cannot hope to experience, is yours at command.

They understand, too, fidelity. When we promise fidelity to Almighty God, what reservations we make at the back of our minds; how clearly it is understood that he must provide us, here and now, with sops of earthly consolation, if he would buy our loyalty! At the altar, where man and woman plight themselves, there is no such hesitancy. "For better, for worse, for richer, for poorer, in sickness and in health, till death do us part"—the voice which trembles over that formula trembles, not from infirmity of purpose, but from depth of emotion.

Be sure of it, this is your hour of grace. This is the moment of clear vision, when you can see the journey that lies before you mapped out, as from a commanding height; there are dusty ways to travel before it is finished, and the summits will be hidden from you. Pray hard to our blessed Lady and St. Joseph that this vision may remain with you; not as a vision still present to your eyes; that is not granted to us; but as a vision remembered, to be the solace of your wayfaring. Remember always that it was a true vision, and you saw it together; you will bear witness to one another that mankind is a better thing than the dull average we see it to be; that life is worth living, and death only a consummation. In that faith, may Almighty God bless and perpetuate in you the sacrament we have celebrated today, and make you, till death and beyond death, one in him.

CHAPTER 24

Life More Abundantly

*I have come so that they may have life,
and have it more abundantly.* (JOHN 10:10)

THERE ARE THREE IMPORTANT MOMENTS IN THE normal human life—birth, marriage, and death; and each of these the Church salutes with a sacrament.

Life is there, but not abundant life, in the child that is brought to the font. It is for the minister of religion to do all that needs doing; the recipient is passive. And when the grace of Extreme Unction seals the passages of sense for the last journey of all, there is life, but not abundant life; the sick man, unconscious perhaps, finds himself in the priest's hands once again. Matrimony is the sacrament of abundant life; youth's powers at the full, youth's ambition still in its first spring-time, youth's ardour, touchwood for the spark of love. The priest? Yes, he

RONALD KNOX

must be there; he is one of the thousand details that must not be overlooked in the hurry of the moment. But he has no real part to play; bride and bridegroom will be the ministers of their own sacrament; they are all-sufficient to each other, and nothing can come between them just now. The Church, for this turn, is content to waive her claim; youth will be served; let them have it so.

Man and woman on their wedding-day are full of abundant life, but they claim, on that day, to have it more abundantly. It is their office, if it be God's will, to hand on the torch of life to another generation. They assume the full status of citizenship; they are to found that cell of humanity, the home; they are to realize, to the full, that enjoyment of companionship which is native to man's genius; they are to know the meaning of that creative afterthought, "It is not good for man to be alone."

In order to have life more abundantly in common, each of them is to accept a curtailment, a diminishing, of the individual life. That is the mysterious law of our being; you must clip the hedge, to make it grow firm; you must sacrifice something on both sides of liberty, of leisure, of inclination, if a partnership is to succeed. Man procures the advantages of a civilized life by a surrender to the State; States live in harmony only at the price of concluding treaties and pacts in which they sign away

Bridegroom and Bride

their liberty. Man and woman on their wedding-day are full of the spirit of self-immolation; "for better, for worse, for richer, for poorer, in sickness and in health"—the lawyer's rigmarole turns into poetry, turns into a love-song, such is their ardour to vanquish one another in the generosity of their giving.

All that, even in the natural order; and in the supernatural order, Christian man and woman on their wedding-day know that their love must go deeper still. They do not come to the altar without bringing a sacrifice. They are reproducing, within narrower limits, that spirit of utter self-abnegation in which our Lord espoused his Church. "With this ring," he said to her, "I thee wed; with this loop of Humanity mysteriously made fast to Godhead. With my body I thee worship; my body broken and bruised and cut to pieces on a cross. And with all my worldly goods I thee endow; my own flesh and blood, for other worldly goods I have none." It is given to you, and with no labour of kindling it, to catch some spark of that divine fire.

"Who can stand close to a blazing fire," asks the *Imitation of Christ*, "and not feel a little of its heat?" Forgive us then, the intrusive friends who gather round you at this focal point of your romance. You must not grudge us the opportunity of warming our hands at your blaze. For

RONALD KNOX

this experienced love of yours is a kind of *gratia gratis data,* put at your disposal, not for your own benefit, but for the benefit of others; *sic vos non vobis...*Charity has turned so cold, these years past; we are chilled, we others, and disillusioned; we must huddle round every watch-fire that gives us leave to remember charity is not dead.

In return, what can we offer you but our prayers; our prayers for both of you, joined now under a single conclusion? We shall wish you, in the well-meaning phrase the world uses, a long life; more intimately we shall wish you, in Jesus Christ's phrase, life more abundantly. For the natural life that now beats in you so strongly is subject to a law of diminishing returns; we are men, and seven times pass over us. If your love were only a function of that natural life, it would be subject to the same fate of impermanence. It is the office of this sacrament to sublimate your natural love, make it into part of that deeper, that more silent stream which feeds the souls of the regenerate; supernatural life. That he, who turned water into wine at the marriage feast, may supernaturalize your love and transform it into a part of the life by which you live to him—that is the least ambition which will satisfy such friends as yours, for such friends as you.

The scenes of every courtship are hallowed by the imagination; yours by historic fact. You have loved,

Bridegroom and Bride

where earth was trodden by divine feet; the walks of our blessed Lady and St. Joseph have been your walks too. May their patronage be with you still, make a Nazareth of your home, and comfort you in the hour of death. And when death disjoins your hands for a little, may they be rejoined still young, still yielded, in heaven.

CLUNY MEDIA

Designed by Fiona Cecile Clarke, the Cluny Media *logo
depicts a monk at work in the scriptorium,
with a cat sitting at his feet.*

*The monk represents our mission to emulate
the invaluable contributions of the monks
of Cluny in preserving the libraries of the West,
our strivings to know and love the truth.*

*The cat at the monk's feet is Pangur Bán, from the
eponymous Irish poem of the 9th century.
The anonymous poet compares his scholarly
pursuit of truth with the cat's happy hunting of mice.
The depiction of Pangur Bán is an homage to the work
of the monks of Irish monasteries and a sign
of the joy we at Cluny take in our trade.*

"Messe ocus Pangur Bán,
cechtar nathar fria saindan:
bíth a menmasam fri seilgg,
mu memna céin im saincheirdd."

Made in the USA
Monee, IL
30 April 2025